The Sun
Star of the Solar System

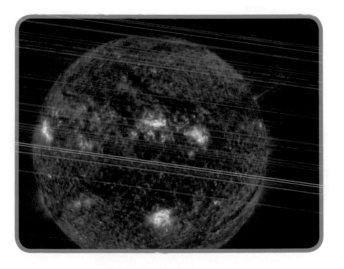

By Lincoln James

Gareth Stevens
Publishing

Please visit our Web site, www.garethstevens.com. For a free color catalog of all our high-quality books, call toll free 1-800-542-2595 or fax 1-877-542-2596.

Library of Congress Cataloging-in-Publication Data

James, Lincoln.
  The sun : star of the solar system / Lincoln James.
    p. cm. — (Our solar system)
  Includes index.
  ISBN 978-1-4339-3849-8 (pbk.)
  ISBN 978-1-4339-3850-4 (6 pack)
  ISBN 978-1-4339-3848-1 (library binding)
  1. Sun—Juvenile literature. I. Title.
  QB521.5.J36 2011
  523.7—dc22

                              2010012654

First Edition

Published in 2011 by
Gareth Stevens Publishing
111 East 14th Street, Suite 349
New York, NY 10003

Designer: Christopher Logan
Editor: Greg Roza

Photo credits. Cover, back cover, pp. 1, 9, 19 Soho (ESA & NASA); pp. 5, 11, 13, 21 Shutterstock.com;
p. 7 Peter Parks/AFP/Getty Images; p. 15 Timm Schamberger/AFP/Getty Images; p. 17 Royal Swedish
Academy of Sciences.

Printed in the United States of America

CPSIA compliance information: Batch #CS10GS: For further information contact Gareth Stevens, New York, New York at 1-800-542-2595.

Contents

Boldface words appear in the glossary.

Our Own Star

The sun is the star at the center of our **solar system**. All the planets in our solar system **orbit** the sun.

Our Solar System

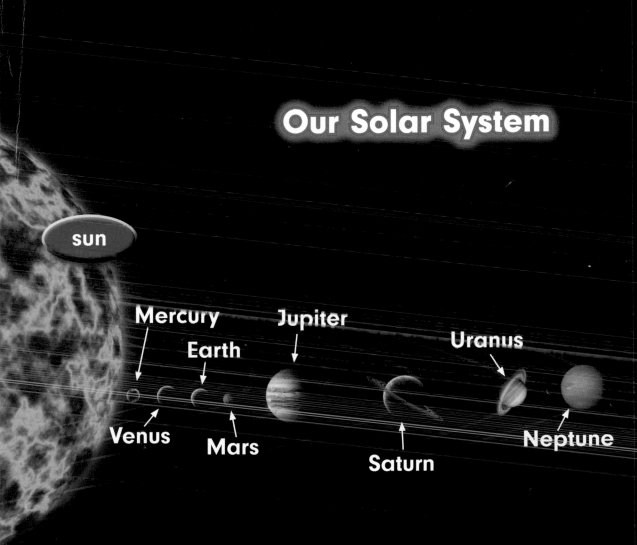

sun

Mercury

Jupiter

Earth

Uranus

Venus

Mars

Saturn

Neptune

The sun is much bigger than any other object in our solar system. Most of the matter in the solar system is in the sun.

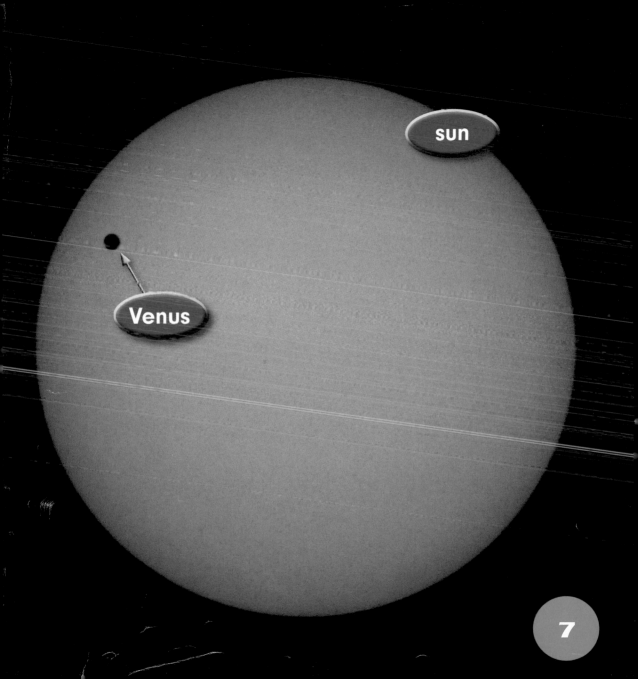

sun

Venus

7

Giant Ball of Gases

Like all stars, the sun is made mostly of the gases hydrogen and helium. Hydrogen is the most common matter in the solar system. Helium is very common, too.

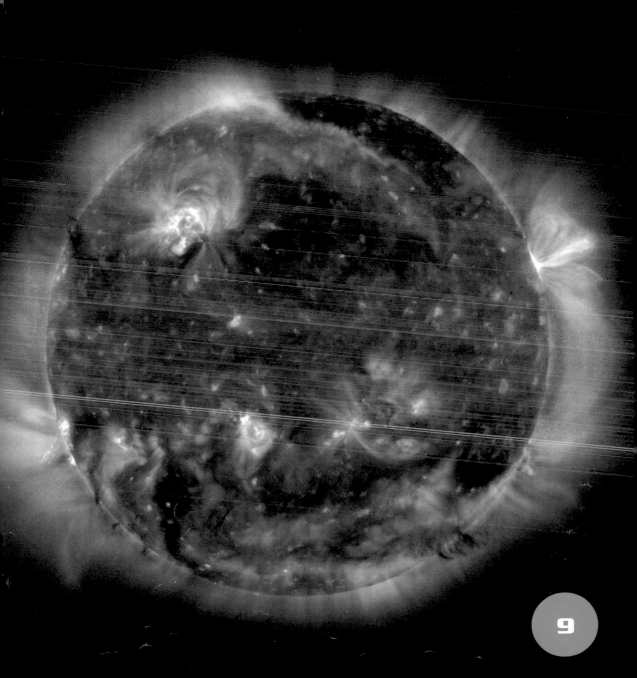

Gravity draws the sun's gases into a tight, hot ball. This causes the hydrogen to change into helium. It also gives off a lot of heat and light.

11

The Sun's Life

The sun is **billions** of years old. It will continue to give off light and heat for a very long time.

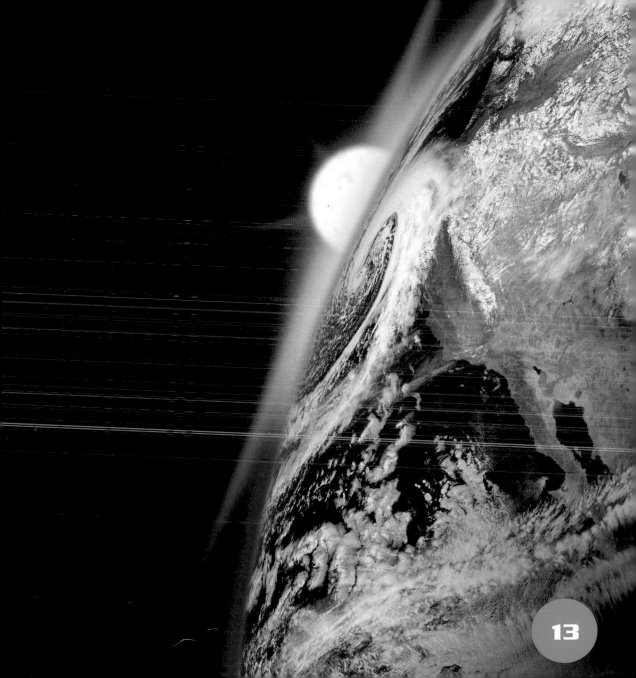

Billions of years from now, the sun will grow much larger and hotter. It will turn red. After that, it will grow smaller and cooler, and turn white.

On the Surface

Dark, cooler areas sometimes form on the sun's **surface**. Scientists call these areas sunspots. One sunspot can be many times larger than Earth!

sunspots

17

Sometimes **explosions** take place on the sun's surface. The explosions shoot giant flames into space.

Star Power!

The sun is our greatest source of **energy**. Earth gets heat and light from the sun. Without the sun, we would not be able to live on Earth.

21

Glossary

billion: 1,000 millions, or 1,000,000,000

energy: power

explosion: a sudden release of energy

gravity: the force that pulls objects toward the center of a planet or star

orbit: to travel in a circle or oval around something

solar system: the sun and all the space objects that orbit it, including the planets and their moons

surface: the top part of a planet, moon, or star

For More Information

Books

Chrismer, Melanie. *The Sun*. New York, NY: Children's Press, 2005.

Eckurt, Edana. *Watching the Sun*. New York, NY: Children's Press, 2004.

Web Sites

The Sun
www.esa.int/esaKIDSen/TheSun.html
Read facts about the sun. Learn how scientists have studied the star of our solar system.

The Sun
www.kidsastronomy.com/our_sun.htm
Read basic facts about the sun. Find links to information about the moons and planets of our solar system, too.

Index

About the Author

Lincoln James is a retired aerospace engineer and amateur astronomer living in St. Augustine, Florida. He enjoys building miniature rockets with his four sons and taking family trips to the Kennedy Space Center to watch space shuttle launches.